THE WASH TO WORCESTER

ROGER SIVITER ARPS

Front Cover: On summer Saturdays until the mid 1980s, the east coast resort of Skegness would play host to many locomotive hauled trains from the East Midlands, Yorkshire and Manchester. On Saturday 16 July 1983, Peak Class 45 No 45007 runs through the attractive station at Havenhouse, some four miles from Skegness, with the 07.32 Sheffield to Skegness train. Note the crossing gates, GNR station buildings and the GNR somersault signal. *Christina Siviter*

Back Cover: With the withdrawal of the English Electric Class 40 locomotives in the early/mid 1980s, several special trains were run throughout the country using these popular locomotives, as on 15 December 1984, when No 40118 is seen entering Worcester Shrub Hill station with the 'Christmas Cracker' special from Bolton to Bristol. *Roger Siviter*

Right: Class 37 No 37019 glows in the late evening sunshine as it departs from the famous Suffolk fishing port and resort town of Lowestoft with the 19.59 train to Norwich on Friday 5 August 1983. Earlier, No 37019 had arrived at Lowestoft with the 16.50 train from London Liverpool Street. A pair of LNER bracket signals and signal box complete this quintessential East Anglian scene. *Roger Siviter*

© Roger Siviter 2005
Published by Great Bear Publishing
34 Shannon Way, Evesham WR11 3FF Tel: 01386 765134
ISBN 0-9541150-4-X

Designed and printed by Ian Allan Ltd, Hersham, Surrey KT12 4RG

Above: On Sunday 24 July 1983, a special charter train, 'The Broadsman', was run from York to London, returning to York via Lowestoft and Norwich with an immaculate Class 40, No 40004, in charge. The return special is seen leaving Lowestoft at Oulton Broad North junction, the lines on the right running to Ipswich and Liverpool Street – the East Suffolk line. (See also picture on page 17.)

Christina Siviter

Opposite: A distinctive feature of the Lowestoft to Norwich line is the swing bridge just to the east of Reedham Junction. On 11 August 1990 a three-car Class 101 Metropolitan – Cammell DMU set crosses over the swing bridge with the 16.50 Lowestoft to Norwich local train. Note the signal box and tall semaphore signal (for sighting purposes).

Roger Siviter

Introduction

'The Wash to Worcester' is the fifth book in the Great Bear Yesteryear Traction series. It is a journey across the heart of England, starting at the famous East Anglian resorts of Lowestoft and Great Yarmouth, and running through the ancient counties of Norfolk and Cambridgeshire, and then heading north to the Skegness line, also calling at the Roman city of Lincoln. From there, we visit the Peterborough area, and then on to Leicester and down the Midland main line to Wellingborough.

Our next location is the former GWR line from Aynho junction to Birmingham, calling briefly on the Oxford – Worcester line and the Stratford upon Avon branch. We then enter Birmingham on the Derby – Leicester line from Water Orton. And finally, we travel from Birmingham to Worcester via the old LMS (via Bromsgrove) route, and the GWR line via Stourbridge Junction.

The period covered is from the mid 1970s to the 1990s, featuring many classes of locomotive that have long ago been made redundant.

In compiling this book, I must thank Hugh Ballantyne and my wife Christina, but most of all the railwaymen who made it all possible.

Roger Siviter, Evesham, 2005

ALSO AVAILABLE IN THIS SERIES

50s WEST – EXETER TO PENZANCE
ISBN 0-9541150-0-7

WATERLOO WEST – WATERLOO TO BARNSTAPLE
ISBN 0-9541150-1-5

SCOTLAND EAST & NORTH
ISBN 0-9541150-2-3

TAUNTON WEST
ISBN 0-9541150-3-1

Author: *Roger Siviter*. Price £14.99

Opposite: On summer Saturdays, the two routes from Norwich to Yarmouth (via both Reedham Junction and Acle) would see a fair amount of locomotive hauled trains, with mainly Class 31s and Class 37s in charge. English Electric Class 37 No 37216 speeds through Reedham Junction station and heads for Great Yarmouth with the 08.00 from Liverpool Lime Street (13.45 ex Norwich). The Class 37 would take over the train at Norwich, the section from Liverpool having been worked by a Class 47 locomotive. 11 August 1990. *Roger Siviter*

Above: This final view at Reedham Junction was also taken on Saturday 11 August 1990, and shows a Metropolitan – Cammell Class 101 DMU as it passes the junction signal box with an early evening Yarmouth to Norwich local train. The bracket signals are of LNER design but the signal box dates from Great Eastern days. Also worth noting (on the right hand side) are the remains of the cattle dock and the fine looking three arched bridge.

Roger Siviter

Opposite and Above: These two views were also taken on Saturday 11 August 1990. The first scene shows Class 47 No 47584, appropriately named *County of Suffolk*, approaching Great Yarmouth station with the ECS of the 11.20 service to London Liverpool Street, the locomotive and stock looking very smart in InterCity livery.

The second picture, taken earlier, shows Class 31 No 31234 in Railfreight Grey livery departing from Great Yarmouth Vauxhall station with the 10.05 train to Liverpool. In the background can be seen the 10.40 train to Birmingham with Class 31 No 31187 in charge, plus an earlier arrival from Liverpool Street and, on the left hand platform, a DMU with a local train to Norwich. Completing this busy summer Saturday scene is the handsome GER signal box and semaphore signals.

Two pictures: Roger Siviter

The northerly route from Great Yarmouth to Norwich (via Brundall junction) runs through the attractive station at Acle. The (Saturdays only) 09.30 Liverpool Street to Great Yarmouth train approaches Acle station with Class 31 No 31224 in charge. The handsome footbridge and station signal box resplendent with flower baskets are a very pleasant reminder of pre-grouping days. 11 August 1990.

Roger Siviter

On 6 August 1983, Class 31 No 31261 enters Brundall junction from the Acle direction with the 10.31 Great Yarmouth to Norwich train, going forward as the 11.15 Norwich to Birmingham New Street. Between the GER signal box and the second carriage can be seen the line running south to Reedham Junction, where the Lowestoft line leaves the other route to Great Yarmouth. The Type 2 Class 31 locomotives were built by Brush, and first introduced in the late 1950s. Until their demise in the late 1990s, they were regular performers in East Anglia, both on passenger and freight workings.

Christina Siviter

Some two miles east of Norwich on the line to Great Yarmouth is Whitlingham, the junction for the branch line to Cromer and Sheringham, a journey of some thirty miles from Norwich. There are still attractive stations on this Great Eastern branch line, including the one at North Walsham where, on Sunday 12 August 1990, a Metropolitan – Cammell Class 101 two-car DMU set No E54079 is seen leaving North Walsham with the 12.55 Sheringham to Norwich train. Note the station buildings and platform canopies, as well as the colourful flower tubs, etc.

The line from Sheringham to Weybourne and Holt, formerly part of the Midland & Great Northern Joint Railway from Cromer to Norwich via Melton Constable, has been preserved. This is known as the North Norfolk Railway, and operates trains throughout most of the year. *Roger Siviter*

Above: Sunday morning at Norwich Thorpe station, 17 July 1983, sees a smart looking Class 47 No 47585 *County of Cambridgeshire* waiting to leave with the 09.27 train to London Liverpool Street. The silver roof of the locomotive denotes that it is probably shedded at Stratford depot. On the right hand side of the picture, beneath the bracket signal, is Norwich Cathedral. Electrification of the London to Norwich route was completed in the mid 1980s and, with it, scenes such as this and the following four pictures would be radically altered, especially with resignalling. *Roger Siviter*

Opposite: This tele-photo picture of part of Norwich Thorpe station and adjacent yard was taken from Carrow Road overbridge on Saturday 6 August 1983. Leaving past Norwich Thorpe signal box is Class 37 No 37110 with the 09.40 to Liverpool Street (ex Great Yarmouth at 08.55). On the right hand side is a Class 47 with the 10.28 service, also to Liverpool Street. Semaphore signals still dominate this busy scene but, as can be seen, electric signalling has made inroads. Completing this picture is a Class 08 on shunting duties, and a pair of Class 37s and a Class 31 locomotive awaiting their next turns of duty. *Christina Siviter*

Above: On 18 September 1975, Class 37 No 37078 pulls out of Norwich Thorpe station with the 13.46 train to Liverpool Street. On the left hand side, Class 03 No 03020 is busy shunting the yard. This picture was also taken from the Carrow Road overbridge, and shows the complete station, plus the spire of Norwich Cathedral. Note the locomotive's split headcodes, one of the many front end variations on the English Electric Class 37s. *Hugh Ballantyne*

Left: In the British Rail summer timetable of 1983, it would be fair to say that the 08.15 Manchester Picadilly to Norwich and Great Yarmouth aroused considerable interest amongst traction enthusiasts, for it would often (but not always) have one of the popular but diminishing band of English Electric Class 40 locomotives in charge. These handsome first generation diesel locomotives, also known as 'Whistlers' (from the sound that they emitted), were first introduced in 1958 and survived until the mid-1980s.

On 6 August 1983, Class 40 No 40080 rounds the tight curve at Norwich Thorpe junction and approaches Thorpe station with the 08.15 from Manchester Picadilly – note the enthusiasts in the front coach! Arrival is scheduled for 12.57 at Norwich – 4 hours 43 minutes for the 215 mile cross country journey which ran via Sheffield, Retford, Peterborough, March and Ely, the train being taken forward to Great Yarmouth (the lines running on the left hand side of the signal box) by either a Class 31 or a Class 37 locomotive. The return working from Norwich to Manchester with No 40080 in charge would leave at 15.11, arriving in Manchester at 21.31, but running via Peterborough, Spalding, Sleaford, Lincoln, Retford and Sheffield. Some day out!

Note also the carriage sidings, beyond which is the station avoiding line. *Christina Siviter*

Opposite: Just over a mile south of Thorpe junction is Trowse Lower junction where the line to London parts company with the line to Ely (for Peterborough and the lines to the Midlands and the North-East as well as the Cambridge and Kings Lynn route).

One of Stratford's immaculate Class 47s, No 47135, is about to pass Trowse Lower junction signal box on 30 August 1980 with a midday Norwich to Liverpool Street train. On the right is the line to Ely which in a short distance will turn west and pass under the London route. At the rear of the train can be seen Trowse station, which closed in the 1960s.

Hugh Ballantyne

Left: We are now on the line to Ely. The location is just west of Thetford station. The train approaching the attractive Great Eastern signal box is our old friend (see page 14) the (Saturdays only) 08.15 Manchester Picadilly to Norwich/Yarmouth, only this time hauled by Class 37 No 37065. These English Electric Type 3 diesel locomotives were built between 1960 and 1965, and a few examples of this long lived class are still to be found at work today on Britain's railway network. They are affectionately known by enthusiasts as 'Growlers'. Also of interest is the loading gauge and small goods platform, both of which are framed by the repeating signal. 23 July 1983. *Christina Siviter*

Opposite: These next two scenes were taken within a few minutes of each other on the evening of Sunday 24 July 1983 at the bridge over the River Ouse at Queen Adelaide, just west of Thetford.

The first picture shows Class 31 No 31412 hurrying westwards with the 18.30 Norwich to Birmingham New Street via Ely North junction, March, Peterborough and Leicester, with arrival in Birmingham at 22.37. During this period, the Class 31s were the mainstay of the Norwich – Birmingham trains.

This second view shows the 'Broadsman' (see picture on page 2) with Class 40 No 40004 in charge on the return journey from Lowestoft to York. Both pictures were taken with kind permission of BR.

Two pictures: Roger Siviter

The Cambridgeshire city of Ely is famous for its splendid mediaeval cathedral and at one time, prior to the electrification of the Liverpool Street to Kings Lynn line, this busy East Anglian junction station was equally as famous amongst railway enthusiasts for its fine selection of semaphore signals and signal boxes.

On the evening of Friday 22 July 1983, a smart looking Class 47 No 47052 passes through a lovely array of semaphore signals as it departs from Ely with the 19.04 Kings Lynn to Cambridge train. Overlooking the scene is Ely South signal box. On the left hand side is the Class 08 yard shunter, and in the down main platform is the rear of a Kings Lynn train.

Roger Siviter

The following morning (23 July 1983) Class 31 No 31217 runs over the crossing at the northern end of Ely station with the 08.27 Peterborough to Harwich train. Once again, a rich variety of semaphore signals plus Ely North signal box and crossing gates add to this East Anglian railway scene.

Christina Siviter

Opposite: Until the electrification in the early 1990s, the London to Kings Lynn trains were worked either by the ubiquitous Brush Class 47s or, as on this occasion, the English Electric Class 37s. On 25 July 1983, Class 37 No 37102 approaches Downham Market station (some ten miles from Kings Lynn) with the 10.35 Liverpool Street to Kings Lynn service.

Controlling the level crossing and station is a fine example of a GER signal box, beyond which is a Victorian mill building. *Christina Siviter*

Above: Our next location is March, situated on the Ely to Peterborough line. Whitemoor goods yard lies just north of March station on the former line to Spalding. March once boasted a busy locomotive shed (31B) with an allocation of around 150 locomotives, including many WD Class 2-8-0s for freight workings. This shed closed in 1963.

On a misty 25 July 1983, Class 31 No 31102 approaches March station with the 09.35 Norwich to Birmingham New Street train. No 31102 was one of a number of Class 31s built without a panel on the front end roof, thus giving them a smoother appearance. Amongst enthusiasts they were popularly known as 'Toffee Apples'! *Christina Siviter*

Left Above: This next picture at March was taken at roughly the same location as the previous scene, only some seven years later, on 9 August 1990. A comparison of the two pictures will show that although the old goods shed, sidings and March East junction signal box are still in situ, all that remains of the station buildings on the right hand side of the older picture is a low wall, with new houses inside the same.

Approaching the camera on that August evening is one of the BREL built Class 56 locomotives No 56103 with the 17.48 March to Mountsorrel Redland empty hopper train. The Class 56 locomotives, which were first introduced in 1976, were withdrawn from service in 2004. *Roger Siviter*

Left Below: Spalding, like many east of England locations, was once a busy junction with lines from Cromer (and Great Yarmouth), March, Peterborough, Melton Mowbray, Sleaford and Boston all converging on the 'Tulip Capital' of England. All that remains today is the through route from Peterborough to Sleaford Junction.

This view, taken at the northern end of Spalding station on 16 July 1983, shows the remains of the goods yard with Class 31 No 31183 on a short ballast train. At the rear of the train by the crossing gates are the remains of the closed line to Boston, and through the mass of semaphore signals can be seen the line to Sleaford. *Roger Siviter*

Opposite: For most people, Skegness is synonymous with holidays, fish and chips, ice cream, etc. but for many traction enthusiasts twenty-odd years ago, it will always be associated with the pairs of English Electric Class 20 locomotives which worked the East Midlands to Skegness summer service trains in those heady far-off days.

On Saturday 16 July 1983, Class 20s Nos 20183 and 20187 wait to depart from Skegness with the (SO) 12.37 to Leicester, having earlier arrived with the (SO) 08.38 from Leicester. Note the small headboard 'Group 20 Chopper Bash', 'Chopper' being the Class 20 locomotive's nickname. One further thing – with the 08.38 arriving in Skegness at 11.26, this would allow Class 20 enthusiasts just over an hour in which to scoff fish and chips, plus ice cream, before the return journey at 12.37! *Roger Siviter*

Above: Turning round from the previous picture (and taken a few minutes earlier) we see Peak Class No 45137 *The Bedfordshire and Hertfordshire Regiment (T.A.)* entering Skegness station with the (SO) 09.22 Derby to Skegness train. Framing this sunny scene is the GNR signal box and a fine looking BR bracket signal, complete with wooden support posts.

Christina Siviter

Opposite: We complete this trio of pictures, taken at the famous east coast resort of Skegness on 16 July 1983, with this telephoto shot of English Electric Class 37 No 37196 as it accelerates away from the station with the (SO) 13.20 train to Manchester Picadilly via Lincoln and Sheffield. Note the two semaphore signals on the left hand side, with GNR and LNER type posts, the further (LNER) being of wooden construction and the nearer (GNR) slotted post being of concrete construction.

Christina Siviter

Some four miles south east of Skegness is the pre-grouping station of Havenhouse, complete with GNR buildings and, at this date (16 July 1983), a fine pair of Great Northern slotted post somersault signals. Approaching the camera in the smart looking BR Blue livery is an unidentified Class 47 locomotive with the (SO) 09.44 Skegness to Kings Cross train, with arrival in the capital at 13.12, 3 hours and 28 minutes being allowed for the 161 mile journey, including seven stops. Note also the attractive rose garden on the right hand side.

Christina Siviter

By the summer of 1990, one of the last few remaining GNR somersault signals in operation on the Skegness line was to be found just to the north west of Thorpe Culvert station, some seven miles from Skegness.

On Saturday 4 August 1990, grey-liveried Class 47 No 47352 is about to pass this splendid pre-grouping signal as it approaches Thorpe Culvert station with the (SO) 10.30 Leeds to Skegness train.

Roger Siviter

Opposite: Our next picture was taken at the ancient Lincolnshire town and port of Boston, some 23¾ miles from Skegness. On 4 June 1980, one of the smallest of the BR diesel fleet, a Class 03 shunter No 03021, propels a train of wagons across the swing bridge into Boston Docks.

These 0-6-0 shunting locomotives were built between 1957 and 1961 at BR Swindon or Doncaster works. They have a tractive effort of 15,300 lbs and a maximum speed of 28 mph. By the end of the 1980s they had been withdrawn from service on BR but many examples are to be found in industry and on preserved lines. Note the signals and the unique octagonal signal box.   *Hugh Ballantyne*

Right: A Metropolitan – Cammell Class 101 two-car DMU forming the (SO) 16.37 Skegness to Doncaster service pulls away fron Sleaford station and approaches Sleaford West signal box (of GNR design) on 4 August 1990. Sleaford is the junction station for Skegness to the east, Spalding and Peterborough to the south, Grantham and Nottingham to the west, and Lincoln to the north.   *Roger Siviter*

Left: The ancient city of Lincoln with its very fine mediaeval cathedral is our next location. On Monday 25 July 1983, English Electric Class 08 0-6-0 shunting locomotive No 08183 is photographed in one of the remaining bay platforms of Lincoln's elegant Central station. This attractive Great Northern station was opened in 1850 and originally had eight platforms, these being reduced to five in recent years. The other main station at Lincoln was St Marks, which served the LMR Nottingham to Grimsby route, but this was closed in 1985, and the Nottingham to Grimsby line trains rerouted via Central station – see picture opposite.

Roger Siviter

Opposite: This second picture at Lincoln was also taken on 25 July 1983, and shows Pelham Street crossing and junction, which is situated just to the east of Lincoln Central station. Rattling over the diamond crossing is an evening Grimsby to Nottingham van train, hauled by an unidentified Class 31 locomotive which in a few yards will run through the (now closed) St Marks station on its journey westwards. The train is crossing over the ex-GNR lines from Lincoln Central station to Boston and Grantham. Note the spur lines on the left hand side which connect trains from Central station to the Grimsby line.

On the right hand side is Pelham Street signal box, and in the background can be seen Sincil Bank signal box, which controlled the crossing gates on the Boston – Grantham line. The line to the left of this box runs to Lincoln diesel depot, which can be seen in the background of the picture. A view of this scene today would show that the line to St Marks station has been taken out, and also that the crossing gates at Sincil Bank are now automated. However, Pelham Street box is still operational, but many of the semaphore signals have gone, and the diesel depot is now closed.

Christina Siviter

Left Above and Below: We are still in Lincolnshire for these next two pictures, but we are now on the East Coast Main Line (ECML), formerly the LNER Kings Cross to Edinburgh route. The first scene was taken at High Dyke near Stoke tunnel on 6 July 1977. A brand new Class 56 No 56032 is seen climbing up the 1 in 200 grade up to Stoke tunnel with a Doncaster to Peterborough test train. In the foreground is the site of the four sidings used to park the iron ore wagons bound for Scunthorpe. The second picture shows English Electric Deltic Class locomotive No 55021 *Argyll & Sutherland Highlander* near Little Bytham with the 14.05 Kings Cross to York train on 2 June 1979.

Two pictures: Hugh Ballantyne

Opposite: On 3 July 1974, Deltic locomotive No 55008 *The Green Howards* is seen passing through the busy station of Peterborough with the 17.00 Kings Cross to Newcastle train. In the background a Class 40, a Class 45 and a Class 25 await their next turns of duty.

The popular English Electric Deltics were first introduced in 1961 as a replacement for the LNER Pacifics on the ECML. There were 22 locomotives in the Class, and there was much sadness amongst enthusiasts when they were all withdrawn from service by 2 January 1982. Happily however, five examples remain in preservation and can sometimes be seen on main line charter trains. *Hugh Ballantyne*

Above: On our railway journey across the heart of England, we now move into Leicestershire and call at Melton Mowbray on the Peterborough to Leicester line. Not only is Melton Mowbray famous for its delicious pork pies, but at Melton station is a fine example of an LMS signal box. Class 37 No 37904 passes Melton signal box and approaches Melton Mowbray station on Thursday 9 August 1990 with an east bound mixed goods train. At the rear of the box is Class 47 No 47205 with a short west bound train of empty hopper wagons, probably bound for Redland Roadstone at Mountsorrel near Barrow-upon-Soar on the Leicester to Loughborough line. Note the overhang of the signal box for sighting purposes for the signalman. *Roger Siviter*

Opposite: Class 31 No 31308, looking smart in the popular BR Blue livery, pulls past Leicester North signal box on Wednesday 15 June 1983 with the 07.40 Norwich to Birmingham New Street train. In the background is the former Midland Railway (MR) goods warehouse.

The Midland main line between Leicester and Loughborough was resignalled by 1988, thus making scenes like this, and the one on the following page, history. *Roger Siviter*

Opposite: This next picture was taken from the other side to the previous view, and shows not only the area around Leicester North box but also the diesel depot, which was on the site of the former Leicester (Midland) steam shed (15A).

Approaching the camera on Saturday 2 July 1983 is Brush Class 47 No 47567 with the 14.14 Norwich to Birmingham New Street service. There is a wonderful variety of semaphore signals to be seen, as well as many Classes of locomotives on the depot, including (according to my records) Class 08s, Class 20s (including No 20153) Class 25s, Class 31s (including No 31204) Class 40 No 40095, a Class 45, Class 46 No 46028 and Class 47s (including No 47525) – a truly fine sight.

Christina Siviter

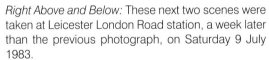

Right Above and Below: These next two scenes were taken at Leicester London Road station, a week later than the previous photograph, on Saturday 9 July 1983.

The first picture shows Class 20s Nos 20183 and 20187 having just arrived with the 12.37 train from Skegness. Note Leicester North signal box at the rear of the train. In the second view, taken a few minutes later, we see Peak Class 45 No 45052 waiting to run south out of the station with the empty stock of the 12.37 from Skegness, the two Class 20s having left the stock and then reversed back to the diesel depot by Leicester North signal box.

Top: Roger Siviter. Bottom: Christina Siviter

Opposite: A pair of Class 31 diesels Nos 31316 and 31154 provide the power for the heavily laden 09.35 Norwich to Birmingham train on 9 July 1983.

The train is seen in the typical urban railway cutting just south of Leicester London Road station, the attractive facade of which can be seen at the rear of the picture. London Road signal box and gantry add to this cityscape, and on the left hand side is the rear of an HST set forming the 11.30 London St Pancras to Sheffield service. With the start of the 1983 summer timetable, the HST units had more or less taken over all the passenger workings from St Pancras to the East Midlands and Sheffield, replacing the popular Peak Class 45 locomotives which had worked on the route since their introduction in 1960. *Christina Siviter*

Above: I mentioned in the previous caption the Class 45 locomotives at work on the Midland main line out of St Pancras, and this picture taken on 6 July 1977 shows them in their prime. No 45107 is seen leaving Market Harborough (some 16 miles south of Leicester) with a down midday train from St Pancras to Nottingham and Sheffield. *Hugh Ballantyne*

Class 45 No 45123 *The Lancashire Fusilier* is about to pass Kettering Station signal box as it pulls out of Kettering on 9 June 1982 with the 16.05 Nottingham to St Pancras train.

The semaphore signals and former Midland Railway signal box would disappear by 1987 with the resignalling program in the area. The photographer is standing on the site of the down goods sidings, which look as though they have recently been removed. Also visible at the rear of the train are the attractive station canopies.

Hugh Ballantyne

On 27 October 1976, Class 25 No 25132 and brake van (their morning's work finished) are seen leaving Twywell for their return journey to Kettering. This iron ore branch was originally part of the MR secondary route from Kettering to Huntingdon and Cambridge. The passenger service on this line finished in 1959, and shortly afterwards the line was truncated at Twywell, leaving a short branch line from there to Kettering to serve the local iron ore traffic. This branch line was closed around 1980.

Hugh Ballantyne

Left Above and Below: These next two pictures were taken at Finedon Road, Wellingborough, on the 14 and 15 of May 1983 respectively, the final weekend of Class 45s working the St Pancras to Leicester and Sheffield trains.

The first scene shows Peak Class No 45103 passing Finedon Road goods yard with a morning Nottingham to St Pancras train, whilst another unidentified member of the Class shunts the yard. Turning round from the previous scene, we see Class 45 No 45137 as it heads north out of Wellingborough with the 18.00 St Pancras to Sheffield train. The diesel depot can be seen in the background, to the right of which is the old steam shed (15A). *Two pictures: Christina Siviter*

Opposite: On 11 May 1983, Class 25 No 25244 is caught by the camera on the up slow line, just north of Wellingborough station, with a south bound ballast train made up of 'Sealion' wagons. Dominating the picture is one of the old steam locomotive sheds, which closed in 1966. Just beyond the shed can be seen the diesel depot, which was built on the site of the other locomotive shed, which was demolished in 1964. Both steam sheds were enclosed round-houses, and in their heyday had an allocation of 70 to 80 mainly freight locomotives, including ex-LMS 8F 2-8-0s and BR Standard Class 9F 2-10-0s.

Hugh Ballantyne

We leave the Midland main line and head westwards to Aynho junction on the former GWR Paddington – Banbury – Birmingham line. On a very sunny January day in 1984 (the 21st) Class 50 No 50016 *Barham* is framed by an attractive bracket signal as it approaches the junction for the Paddington and Oxford lines with the 08.20 Liverpool Lime Street to Paddington via Birmingham New Street and Banbury. The English Electric Class 50s were first introduced in 1967, and were withdrawn from service by 1992. These popular locomotives were regular performers on this route between the mid 1970s and 1990. Note the mixture of upper and lower quadrant signals. This was brought about by regional changes in the area.

Roger Siviter

Unlike the Class 50s, the Class 58 locomotives were comparative newcomers to BR, having been built between 1983 and 1987 by BREL at Doncaster Works. However, they had a shorter life than some Classes of diesel locomotives, most of the Class having been withdrawn by 2002. No 58047 in Railfreight Grey livery is seen just north of Kings Sutton, some three miles south of Banbury, with an up coal train, on Monday 6 May 1991.

Roger Siviter

Class 47 No 47501 passes the gas works as it heads out of the famous old market town of Banbury on 21 January 1984 with the 10.23 Manchester Picadilly to Brighton train via Reading and East Croydon, with an arrival at the south coast resort at 16.20.

The area behind the photographer (which is just south of Banbury station) was where Banbury locomotive shed (84C later 2D) was situated. This depot, which had an allocation of 70 locomotives in 1950, had dwindled to around 20 locomotives, mainly 'Black 5' 4-6-0s, 8F 2-8-0s and Standard Class 9F 2-10-0s, by the time it was closed in the latter part of 1966. *Christina Siviter*

This view at the north end of Banbury station was also taken on 21 January 1984, and shows station pilot Brush Type 2 Class 31 locomotive No 31295 awaiting its next turn of duty in the down bay platform. Note the old platform trolleys, probably dating from GWR days.

The original station at Banbury had an overall wooden roof, but this was demolished in 1952 and replaced with two platform awnings, but all the old station was demolished in 1956 to make way for the new concrete and brick station, which was built in 1958 during the BR modernisation plan of that period.
Roger Siviter

We leave the Banbury to Birmingham line for the time being to look at the Oxford to Worcester line, which today is known as the Cotswold line. Originally, the line ran to Wolverhampton and was affectionately known as the OWW, or 'Old Worse and Wear'! This northern section of the line was truncated at Round Oak (Brierley Hill) in March 1993.

Throughout the 1980s, the popular Class 50 locomotives could often be seen on the Paddington to Worcester and Hereford service, as well as on Sunday diversion trains using the route. On Sunday 25 September 1983, Class 50 No 50039 *Implacable* enters Moreton in Marsh station with the diverted 08.50 Paddington to Glasgow train. As can be seen, this attractive station in the heart of the beautiful Cotswolds still had a GWR signal box and semaphore signals, and indeed it is still the same today.

Christina Siviter

Although the Class 50s were withdrawn by 1992, several examples were preserved and occasionally can be seen on the Oxford to Worcester line, as on Saturday 4 September 1999, when No 50031 *Hood* and D444 (formerly No 50044 *Exeter*) head a Reading to York charter train over the Avon river bridge, as they approach the picturesque Worcestershire market town of Evesham, set in the Vale of Evesham on the western edge of the Cotswold hills. Both these powerful English Electric locomotives were preserved by the 'Fifty Fund' when they were withdrawn from BR in 1991, and are based on the Severn Valley Railway (SVR) at their Kidderminster depot. *Roger Siviter*

We now return to the old GWR main line between Banbury and Birmingham. The location is Harbury cutting, some 14 miles north of Banbury.

It is 1.30 p.m. on a beautiful early spring day, Saturday 23 March 1991, as

Class 58 No 58013 climbs the 1 in 143 up to Harbury tunnel with a heavy up coal train (MGR) bound for Didcot power station.   *Roger Siviter*

These days, a lot of the freight traffic from the Birmingham area to Southampton travels between Leamington Spa and Birmingham via Kenilworth and Coventry, thus missing out the GWR route from Leamington to Birmingham via Hatton bank. And so, I hope, this photograph taken on the evening of Sunday 13 May 1989 will be a pleasant reminder of freight traffic on Hatton bank. The location is just east of Hatton station approaching the lovely three-arch road bridge, and the train is a Lawley Street to Southampton Freightliner service, hauled by Class 47 No 47116. Note the three tracks, the far line being used by Stratford upon Avon trains, the junction for this line being just to the west of Hatton station.

Roger Siviter

Left: After 1976, when the through route between Stratford upon Avon and Cheltenham was closed, leaving Stratford as the terminus for both the lines from Birmingham and Hatton, the sighting of a freight train on the Stratford line must have been a rare occurrence. However, Sunday 13 September 1981 was one of those lucky days, when Class 25 No 25034 (off Bescot depot) was caught by the camera as it climbed out of Stratford near Bishopton with an empty ballast train, bound for the Birmingham area. The Class 25 locomotives (known affectionately as 'Rats') were first introduced in 1961 and built by BR at their Crewe, Darlington and Derby works, and remained in service until the mid-1980s. Several members of the Class have been preserved. *Christina Siviter*

Opposite: Our final picture on the ex-GWR Leamington to Birmingham line shows a winter's day at Lapworth as Class 50 No 50034 *Furious* heads for Leamington Spa with the ECS of a VSO Pullman train which had earlier worked into Leamington from Paddington, the stock being stored at Tyseley sidings, prior to the return trip to Paddington. Note that the main line from Tyseley to Lapworth was once four track, being reduced to two track around 1970. 16 February 1983. *Christina Siviter*

We are now on the eastern outskirts of the Birmingham area at Water Orton. This location is not only the junction for the lines to Derby to the north and Leicester to the east but also, for many years right through from steam days to the present day, it has been popular with enthusiasts, especially spotters, who are often to be seen perched on that lengthy wall.

On 6 May 1987, Class 58 No 58033 approaches Water Orton with a west bound coal train from the Derby direction. The line from Leicester can be seen on the right hand side of the picture. At the rear of the picture is Hams Hall power station, which was demolished some years ago, and the area is now a freight terminal.

Roger Siviter

Turning round from the previous picture, we get a view of the old Water Orton East Junction signal box and the eastern end of the station with its fine looking Midland Railway design entrance and booking hall.

The train, hauled by Class 31 No 31408, is the 14.20 Birmingham New Street to Peterborough and Norwich service. By this date, 6 May 1987, the old signal box was used as a tool store, and remained so until it was demolished in the summer of 1999. The Class 31s worked the Birmingham to Norwich trains until the late 1980s, when the Class 158 Sprinter units took over their duties on the route.

Roger Siviter

Left: On Sunday afternoon, 3 May 1992, Class 47 No 47219 runs through the site of Castle Bromwich station, some two miles west of Water Orton, with a ballast train probably bound for Saltley depot.

Out of sight behind the trees on the left hand side is Castle Vale estate, which in the early post war years was the site of the British Industries Fair (BIF). This was usually held in May of each year, and neccessitated many extra trains calling at Castle Bromwich station for the event. Note the out-of-use sidings on the right hand side beneath a small cement terminal. *Roger Siviter*

Opposite: This next photograph was taken on the afternoon of Tuesday 14 April 1982 at Bromford Bridge on the Birmingham to Derby/Leicester line, a mile east of Saltley, where the elevated section of the M6 motorway runs parallel with the railway.

Class 08 No 08068 is seen shunting near Stewarts & Lloyds, Ltd. Bromford Tube Works. This works had its own internal railway and industrial locomotives (originally steam, and latterly diesel), together with exchange sidings with BR. But all this was demolished after closure of the factory in the 1990s. *Christina Siviter*

This picture was also taken at Bromford Bridge on the same day as the previous scene, and shows Class 45 No 45057 approaching the camera with a Birmingham to Derby train, probably a Bristol to Newcastle service. This wider view also shows the extensive goods sidings and, on the right hand side, the cooling towers of Neachells power station (demolished around 1990). On the left hand side is the edge of Saltley gas works, whilst dominating the scene is the M6 motorway with what appears to be only a fraction of the traffic on it compared to today.

Christina Siviter

Class 47 No 47310 *Raven* is seen at Saltley on 5 May 1990, backing a Southampton to Lawley Street (Birmingham) Freightliner train. After reversing the stock into the goods depot, the locomotive will then run to the nearby Saltley diesel depot for servicing. This depot was built on the site of the old Saltley steam shed (21A) which closed in 1966. This large former Midland Railway locomotive shed consisted of three round houses. The present day diesel depot spans the site of the old No 1 shed, with factory units now standing on the site of the other sheds.

Hugh Ballantyne

We are now in central Birmingham at the former GWR Moor Street station. This attractive terminus station was opened in 1909 and was mainly used as a suburban station for the north Warwickshire area. It was closed in 1987, shortly after the opening of the new through station (to Snow Hill) which was built by the side of the old station. Happily though, after many years the old station has been beautifully restored to its original condition and is now a Heritage Site, and in the not too distant future it will, hopefully, be used by special steam and diesel charter trains. When this picture was taken on 13 November 1985, Moor Street station was still a fairly busy suburban station, with a three car DMU set waiting to enter platform 3 with the 12.10 to Stratford upon Avon when the 11.40 service to Shirley (out of sight behind the Stratford train) has departed.

Roger Siviter

It would be fair to say that during daylight hours the modern Birmingham New Street station is not the most attractive of stations in which to photograph trains. However, at night time it is a far more photogenic location, witness this photograph taken on the evening of 24 January 1983, showing Class 25 No 25123 at platform 9 of this vast station with a south bound parcels train.

Roger Siviter

Opposite: We leave Birmingham and travel down the former LMS line to Bromsgrove and Droitwich (for Worcester). The route runs roughly parallel with the Worcester & Birmingham canal as far as Bournville, passing by the University of Birmingham and through University station, which opened in 1978. On 25 January 1984, Class 47 No 47600 runs by the side of the canal and heads for New Street station with the 07.05 Plymouth to York service. At the rear of the train can be seen the then new University station and also, through the trees on the right hand side, part of the large university complex. This section of the line is now electrified as far as Barnt Green, junction for the Redditch branch line and roughly the top of the famous Lickey Bank.

Roger Siviter

Above: Class 46 No 46004 climbs up to Kings Norton station with a special excursion train, probably bound for the south-west coastal resort of Paignton, on Whit Monday the 29 May 1983. On the right is the Camp Hill relief line. This line is mainly used for freight traffic, with some use by passenger traffic on summer Saturdays. From this location to Barnt Green the track is quadruple.

The Class 46 locomotives were first introduced in 1961, and were a development of the Peak (45) Class. They were withdrawn from service by the mid 1980s, but happily several examples of the Class have been preserved, including No 46035, which has been employed on main line charter trains.

Christina Siviter

A fine sight at Blackwell on the early evening of Tuesday 29 May 1997, as a trio of English Electric Class 37 locomotives Nos 37244, 37255 and 37254 cautiously descend the approach to the Lickey Bank with a train of brand new coal wagons, bound for the Cardiff area.

I am standing on the site of Blackwell station where in steam days the banking locomotives, not being coupled to the train, would leave the train and then run down the bank to Bromsgrove to await their next duty. *Roger Siviter*

I mentioned in the previous caption the work of the Lickey Bankers. When steam finished on the route at the end of the summer timetable of 1964, Bromsgrove locomotive shed was also closed, and the banking duties for many years were taken over by pairs of Class 37s, shedded at the remains of Worcester depot. On the frosty morning of 18 February 1983, No 37180 *Sir Dyfed/County of Dyfed* and No 37270 bank a freight up the 1 in 37 of the Lickey Incline. The train is hauled by Class 25 No 25154, and the location is Vigo Bridge, half a mile south of the site of Blackwell station.   *Christina Siviter*

Above: Our next location is just south of Bromsgrove station where, at 12.35 p.m. on Saturday 17 October 1992, a quintet of Class 47 locomotives appeared, heading for the Birmingham area.

The first locomotive is No 47574 *Benjamin Gimbert G.C.,* the second No 47481, the third unidentified, the fourth engine is No 47843 and the fifth locomotive of this perhaps unique sight is also unidentified. The three different locomotive liveries also make interesting comparisons. *Roger Siviter*

Opposite: One of the enjoyments of living at Bromsgrove, especially at Stoke Heath just south of the town, was that when the weather was fine, or as in the case of the picture overleaf, very wintry with thick snow, being able to nip out of the house and within a mile or so being in a photogenic position on the Birmingham to Bristol main line. On summer Saturdays in the late 1980s, pairs of Class 31 locomotives could be seen with holiday trains from the Manchester area to the Torbay seaside resorts, and of course vice versa.

On the penultimate summer Saturday of the 1989 summer timetable, 23 September, Class 31s Nos 31466 and 31426, looking a treat in the BR Blue livery, hurry downgrade near Stoke Prior (just south of Bromsgrove) with the 09.33 Stockport to Paignton train. *Roger Siviter*

At the same location as the picture on the previous page, but this time on a very wintry day – 8 February 1991 – we see Class 47 No 47316 *Wren* heading south with a Birmingham Longbridge to Swindon freight service.

The fall of snow was fresh that morning, but as was commonplace in the Bromsgrove area, certainly around that time, it would all be gone after a few days.

Roger Siviter

This winter picture was taken some years before the previous scene, on 25 January 1984. The location is Rood End sidings at Langley on the former GWR Birmingham to Stourbridge route. Class 31 No 31171 is seen shunting chemical tank wagons, which it has just worked out of Allbright & Wilson chemical works on the right hand side. Note the mixture of upper and lower quadrant semaphore signals, due to regional changes. Unlike the Midland route from Birmingham to Droitwich (via Bromsgrove) which once outside the Birmingham suburbs passes through mainly rural areas, the ex-GWR route runs through the industrial 'Black Country' as far as Stourbridge, passing through Smethwick, Oldbury/Langley, Rowley Regis, Old Hill, Cradley Heath and Lye, before arriving at Stourbridge Junction.

Roger Siviter

In complete contrast to the previous scene (the location of which is just beyond the road bridge), on Saturday 14 April 1984, a Class 108 DMU unit approaches Langley Green station with the 16.38 Birmingham New Street to Stourbridge Junction train. Dominating the scene is a fine example of a GWR bracket signal. Behind the photographer is the GWR signal box which controlled the area, but alas the box and signals have now all been replaced.

The line on the left hand side ran into the original Oldbury station and on to Oldbury goods station. The passenger station closed in 1915, but the goods station remained open until the mid 1980s. This route originally ran to Birmingham Snow Hill station until its closure in 1972. Then, until the new Snow Hill station was opened in 1987, it ran into New Street station.

Christina Siviter

70

Another 'Black Country' scene, although this view, taken at Rowley Regis on the morning of 14 April 1984, somewhat contradicts that. The train is a 'Footex' special from Plymouth to Birmingham Witton, conveying fans of Plymouth Argyle Football Club to Villa Park for the semi-final of the FA cup. This train is appropriately hauled by one of Laira's Class 50 locomotives, No 50010 *Monarch*. The train was one of eleven specials that ran that day from Plymouth to Witton, six travelling via the Bromsgrove line and the rest via Stourbridge Junction; all the trains were hauled by Class 50s. At the rear of the train (just out of sight) is the entrance to Old Hill tunnel.

On a football note, despite the presence of 20,000 Argyle fans (nearly four times their average attendance), sadly the Third Division side lost 1-0 to First Division Watford.

Christina Siviter

Opposite: Although Stourbridge Junction has long lost its semaphore signals, it still retains its impressive signal box. Approaching the same on Sunday 1 July 1990 is Class 56 No 56034 with a special charter train which left Birmingham New Street at 11.00 and ran through to Bristol Temple Meads. This was one of a series of specials which were run that day (in connection with Gloucester's Open Day) between Birmingham and Bristol (and return), and was organised by one of the country's leading railway charter companies – Pathfinder Tours of Woodchester, Gloucestershire. *Roger Siviter*

Right Above: This view at Stourbridge Junction was taken on Wednesday 18 January 1984, and shows English Electric Class 40 No 40195 running into the junction station after shunting in the yard, which is situated behind the signal box. At the rear of the locomotive are the lines to Birmingham and Dudley, which part company about half a mile north of the station. Off the left of the picture is the short branch line to Stourbridge Town station, which is worked by a single-car DMU. *Roger Siviter*

Right Below: At Droitwich Spa, the two lines from Birmingham (both via Bromsgrove and Stourbridge Junction) meet and then run on to Worcester.

On Sunday 25 September 1983, Class 47 No 47351 runs into Droitwich from the Bromsgrove direction with the diverted 10.55 Manchester Picadilly to London Paddington train. The normal route for this service is via Leamington Spa and Banbury, but today it will run through Worcester Shrub Hill and down the Cotswold line to Oxford, and then on to Paddington. Note the busy looking coal yard on the right hand side, which at the time had its own diesel locomotive, the back of which can just be seen parked behind the railway huts. The coal yard and locomotive have now all gone but happily, however, the signal box and signals still remain.

Christina Siviter

Turning round from the previous picture, we see Class 47 No 47453 as it runs through Droitwich Spa station on Sunday 19 April 1987 with the diverted 09.44 Reading to Birmingham New Street train.

Although some of the GWR station buildings have been replaced, there is still a GWR waiting room on the south bound platform and also well kept station gardens on both platforms.

Christina Siviter

Class 47 No 47814 in InterCity livery, plus seven matching coaches, runs downgrade to Rainbow Hill tunnel, just to the north of Worcester Shrub Hill station, with the 08.56 Liverpool Lime Street to Poole train, running via Birmingham, Worcester, Oxford and Reading. To the south of the tunnel is Worcester Tunnel junction, where the lines to Shrub Hill station and Foregate Street station (for Hereford) split. The date is Sunday 2 October 1993. *Roger Siviter*

Left: Sunday 2 May 1993 was a Worcester Open Day, and as well as special shuttle trains running between Shrub Hill station across the River Severn to Rushwick, a special charter train from Worcester to Hereford was run, hauled by a pair of English Electric Type 1 Class 20s Nos 20038 and 20066. The special is seen here crossing over the River Severn bridge at Worcester on its outward journey. *Roger Siviter*

Opposite: During the 1980s, the Paddington – Worcester – Hereford trains were hauled by Class 50s, and latterly by Class 47 locomotives. On 7 May 1989, Class 47 No 47583 *County of Hertfordshire*, in Network South East livery, has just left Shrub Hill station and heads down the bank to Worcester Foregate Street station with the (Su.O) 13.45 Paddington to Hereford service. The waterway is the Birmingham to Worcester canal. *Roger Siviter*

Above: In splendid evening sunshine, English Electric Class 50 No 50010 *Monarch* looks a treat as it pulls out of Worcester Shrub Hill station with the 16.10 Paddington to Hereford service on Sunday 19 April 1987. The popular Class 50 locomotives finished work on this route in the spring of 1989.

Roger Siviter

Opposite: By standing on the northern end of Shrub Hill station, you get a fine view of the many signals, and also (at the time of the photograph, 19 April 1987) part of the old steam shed (85A) then used as a diesel depot and stabling point. Approaching the camera on this lovely spring evening is Class 47 No 47622 with the 16.15 Hereford – Worcester – Paddington service. To the right of the train are the lines to Droitwich Spa.

Roger Siviter

Our final picture was taken on the evening of 5 January 1984, and shows Peak Class 45 No 45057 waiting to leave Worcester Shrub Hill station with the 15.35 Leeds to Bristol parcels train. Note the attractive platform awnings and support poles.

Roger Siviter